Y0-AAZ-301

A gift for
_____

From

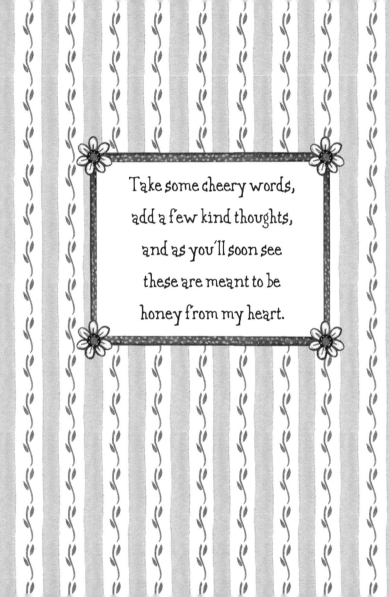

Take some cheery words,
add a few kind thoughts,
and as you'll soon see
these are meant to be
honey from my heart.

Honey from My Heart
for You, Friend

Illustrated by Debra Jordan Bryan

COUNTRYMAN

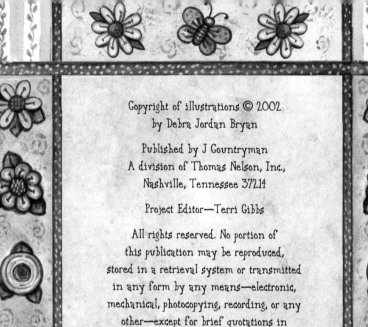

Published by J Countryman
A division of Thomas Nelson, Inc.,
Nashville, Tennessee 37214

Project Editor—Terri Gibbs

Designed by Left Coast Design,
Portland, Oregon

ISBN: 0-8499-9531-0

www.jcountryman.com
www.thomasnelson.com

Printed in U. S. A.

A friend is
someone you
like to BEE with.
Someone BEARY special!!

Happiness is
like honey, . . .
it's more fun
when shared.

You can search the wide world over, like bees buzzing around clover, . . .

only to learn
that you really discover
your true self
in the heart of a friend.

The day is so much
more friendly
when I can spend it with you.

Some favorite things for us to do:

_____

_____

_____

Love is the gift
of yourself.

Love begins
in the heart,
that's where
it starts,
but when you
give it away,
somehow...
it lasts all day!

I thank God
upon every
remembrance
of you.

Philippians 1:3

When looking for
a truly good friend,
making haste
will never do.
You must browse until
your heart's content.
I know, for that's
how I found you!

If there were
more people in
the world like you,
there'd be
more hugs and
laughter too!

friends at home
who love you,
friends
elsewhere
who miss
you, . . .

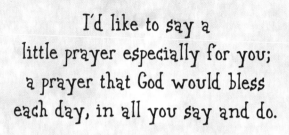

I'd like to say a
little prayer especially for you;
a prayer that God would bless
each day, in all you say and do.

Debra Jordan Bryan

A little prayer for you:

_____

_____

_____

_____

_____

_____

_____

Just want
you to know
you'll always BEE
a BEARY special
friend to me.

"Come have tea in the garden with me."

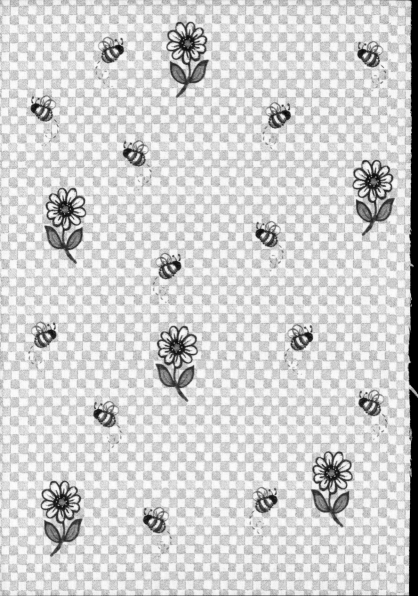